The Gingerbread Man

LEVEL A

A Publication of the World Language Division

Editor-in-Chief: Judith Bittinger

Project Director: Elinor Chamas

Editorial Development: Elly Schottman

Production/Manufacturing: James W. Gibbons

Cover and Text Design/Art Direction: Taurins Design Associates, New York

Illustrator: John Sandford

ISBN 0-201-19054-0
9 10 11 12 13 14 15-WR-96 95 94 93

Addison-Wesley Publishing Company

Reading, Massachusetts • Menlo Park, California • New York • Don Mills, Ontario • Wokingham, England
Amsterdam • Bonn • Sydney • Singapore • Tokyo • Madrid • San Juan

Once upon a time,
a  made a .

When she opened
the oven door,
out jumped the !

Away he ran.
"Stop!" cried the .
But the  just laughed.

"Run, run, run,
    As fast as you can.
    You can't catch me,
    I'm the ."

5

The  ran past a field.
He saw a .
"Stop!" cried the .
But the  just laughed.

6

"Run, run, run,
   As fast as you can.
   You can't catch me,
   I'm the ."

The  ran into the woods.
He saw a  .
"Stop!" cried the  .
But the  just laughed.

"Run, run, run,
   As fast as you can.
   You can't catch me,
   I'm the  ."

Then the 🍪 came
to a river.
He saw a 🐊.

"Please, Mr. 🐊,
take me across the river,"
said the 🍪.
"Certainly, little 🍪,"
said the 🐊.
"Just climb on my nose."

"Come back," said the 🧒 .
"Come back," said the 👨 .
"Come back," said the 🐕 .

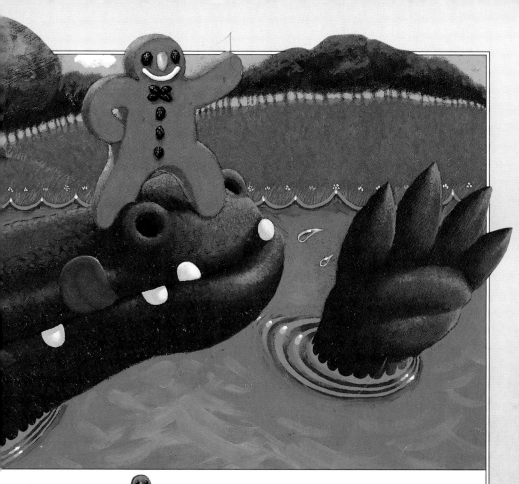

But the just laughed.
The swam away
with the on his nose.

When they came to the
middle of the river, the
 said,
"Good-bye, little !"
The  opened his
mouth and **SNAP! GULP!**

That was the end
of the  !